CW00384693

paines PLOUGH

Crazyhorse

by Parv Bancil

CRAZYHORSE began life as a short play, written for the Paines Plough Writers' Group Season of rehearsed readings, THE WILD LUNCH, at the Bridewell Theatre, London, in March 1997.

This development of writing talent from workshops to rehearsed readings and to final production is a crucial aspect of Paines Plough's work. It is through this long-term commitment to writers that we are able to encourage new and distinctive voices for the stage and that audiences around the country can benefit from their work.

We believe Parv Bancil is one such writer, with a unique view of contemporary British society and the ability to create a good story. We are therefore delighted to present CRAZYHORSE by Parv Bancil and hope you enjoy it.

Vicky Featherstone, Artistic Director

FUNDED BY

LONDON
BOROUGHS
GRANTS
COMMITTEE

This programme/playscript went to press while the play was still in rehearsal, and the text in performance may differ in some respects from that printed here.

SUPPORTED BY
THE NATIONAL LOTTERY
THROUGH
THE **ARTS COUNCIL**
OF ENGLAND

**LONDON
ARTS BOARD**

Funded by
THE
**ARTS
COUNCIL**
OF ENGLAND

Paines Plough

With an impressive new artistic team at its core, Paines Plough has entered a dynamic new era and is set to produce some of its most consistently exciting work to date for audiences around the country.

Since 1974 we have been commissioning and developing work by some of the country's greatest writers, including Stephen Jeffreys, Terry Johnson, Pam Gems, Doug Lucie, Christina Reid, Rona Munro, Nick Dear and April de Angelis.

Our reputation has been built on the belief that the writer's voice is an integral part of society – their ideas and views enrich our lives, challenging us to think about the world and times we live in.

We commission writers, encouraging them to take risks, in collaborations with the artistic team – to find the most adventurous and fulfilling ways to communicate to their audience. But these ideas are nothing without the ability to tell a good story, a story that will engross and amuse, stimulate and inspire.

Tara Arts

In the twentieth year of producing innovative theatre, Tara Arts remains determinedly committed to bringing an Asian sensibility to British theatre. This commitment is manifest in diverse theatre-works, for highly diverse audiences, with texts ranging from the classics of European and Indian theatre to contemporary plays from Britain and India. As part of Tara's sensibility, the company plans to extend its diversity through producing stories on multi-media formats. These include talking books and multi-media CDs. These are seen as necessary extensions of the company's Internet presence.

In 1997 alone the company has produced a distinctive version of Shakespeare's *Midsummer Night's Dream* for children, BOTTOM'S DREAM; a first play from a new Asian writer, OH SWEET SITA by Ravi Kapoor; and a modern Indian play, DANCE LIKE A MAN, by Mahesh Dattani. We are delighted to end the year with this co-production with Paines Plough of Parv Bancil's CRAZYHORSE and its unique view of Asian life in contemporary Britain.

Paines Plough *and* **Tara Arts**

present the world premiere of

CRAZYHORSE

by Parv Bancil

Jas	Ameet Channa
Nobby	Jonathan McGuinness
Mr Jutla	Madhav Sharma
Ronnie	Laurence Stevenson
Linda	Tracy Wiles

Director	Vicky Featherstone
Designer	Neil Warmington
Lighting Designer	Ian Scott
Sound Designer	Mike Furness

Production Management	Alison Richie Associates
Company Stage Manager	Tania Peach
Stage Manager	Neil Gavin
Production Photos	Franca Chretien
Press Representatives	Cameron Duncan
	0171 383 0866
Marketing	Jackie Ellman
	0171 829 8465

The play is set in the present time, in a lock-up garage at the back of Mr Jutla's house, and takes place over the course of a day.

First performance October 1st 1997 at the New Vic Studio, Bristol Old Vic. Press night October 3rd.

Biographies

Parv Bancil – Writer

Parv was born in Tanzania and came to England two years later to settle in Hounslow. He left school at 16 and became a DJ for two years. After a stint in a sun tan lotion factory, he got his first job in theatre when he joined Hac Theatre as their Stage Manager. When the company ran into difficulties, Parv and a couple of actors took over and produced their own work. Parv co-wrote his first play with Ravinder Gill called CURSE OF THE DEAD DOG. The play focussed on British Asian experiences, which soon became the company's agenda and indeed the driving force behind Parv's work. At a time when much Asian theatre was concentrating on adaptations of classics and plays that were vehicles for political views; Parv was looking at the lives and futures of 'real' British Asian characters who, although products of this country, neither belonged to it nor their original place of descent. He wrote about the immediacy of their situations and the sub-cultures that they were exposed to.

Parv won the Young Playwrights Festival for BBC Radio 4 in 1991 and completed a residency at the Royal Court in 1996. He is currently developing a short story for Carlton TV and a new play for Yehlellah Theatre in Birmingham.

His plays include HOW'S YOUR SKULL? DOES IT FIT?, KINGS, BAD COMPANY for Hac Theatre, BLOODLINE for Tara Arts, THE BROTHERHOOD for Yehlellah Theatre, UNGRATEFUL DEAD for Watermans, NADIR for BBC Radio 4 and JAGO. (GET REAL) for Peshkar Theatre.

Apart from serious drama, Parv has also been active within the comedy scene of 'One Nation Under a Groove . . . innit' with the 'Sycophantic Sponge Bunch' and the 'Dead Jellebies'.

Ameet Channa – Jas

Ameet trained at the London Academy of Acting.
Theatre; READY OR NOT, DUSKY WARRIORS (Stratford East), SKELETON (Soho Theatre Company, UNGRATEFUL DEAD, BAD COMPANY, GIRLIES, (Watermans Art Centre), EAST IS EAST (Royal Court Workshop), VOICES IN THE WIND, WICKED YAAR! (Royal National Theatre), AN IMMIGRANT'S SONG (Cars in Water), BEHIND THE VEILED FACE (Whispering Eyes), THE DICE GAME (Nottingham Playhouse), CRUCIFER OF BLOOD, (PW Productions).
TV; THE ACCUSED (BBC Series), DEAR DILEMMA (LWT), THE BILL (Thames), TEENAGE HEALTH FREAKS II (Limelight Productions), PROSPECT STREET (Wyverne TV).
Film; THE DRIVE (Take Away), WILD WEST (Initial Films), PRINCELET OF GOLUM STREET (NFTS).
Radio includes; HOUSE OF SUN, UGANDA, GIRLIES, SCORCHING WINDS (BBC), LIFE OF KRISHNA (Right Angle).

Jonathan McGuinness – Nobby

Jonathan trained at Central School of Speech & Drama.
Theatre includes; THE LOVE OF A GOOD MAN, ROSA CARNAVORA (Arts Threshold), THE TAMING OF THE SHREW (Ludlow Festival), THE KNOCKY, THE CORNER BOYS (Royal Court Theatre Upstairs), LOOT (Latchmere Theatre), THE REVENGER'S TRAGEDY (Orange Tree Theatre), CHAMPION OF PARIBANOU (Steven Joseph Th, Scarborough), CRACKED EGGS (Finborough Arms, New Play Writing Festival), TWO WEEKS WITH THE QUEEN (Leicester Haymarket).
TV; A LITTLE PATCH OF GROUND, THE SOLDIER (BBC TV), LITTLE NAPOLEONS, GAME ON (Hat Trick), SHARPE'S GOLD (Central TV), CROWN PROSECUTOR (BBC TV), GET CALF – COOGABER PROAN'S RUN (Pozzitive Productions, POLDARK (BBC TV). THE BILL, MY GOOD FRIEND, HAVE YOUR CAKE AND EAT IT.

Madhav Sharma – Mr Jutla

Involvement in new writing includes work by Tom Stoppard, Dharmesh Chauhan, Michael Wall, Parminder Sekhon & Shakila Maan, Paul Sirrett, Meira Chand, Gareth Jones & Victoria Hine, Amina Osman, David Mowat, Tanika Gupta, John Matthews, Mark Tully, R.K.Narayan, Harwant Bains, David Edgar, Girish Karnad, Howard Barker, Neil Biswas, Richard Edmunds, Deepak Verma, Terry James, Michael Sharp, David Fitzsimmons, Royce Ryton, Bill Morrison, Bill Lyons, Lynda Marchal, Guy Roderick & Peter Cox, Nandita Ghose and Steve Walker. A lover of Shakespeare (he played the title role in HAMLET directed by Joseph O'Conor), Madhav lives in a thatched Cottage in Suffolk.

Laurence Stevenson – Ronnie

Laurence trained at the Central School of Speech and Drama. Theatre includes; RHINOCEROS (Brixton Shaw Theatre), READY OR NOT (Theatre Royal, Stratford East), ENEMY OF THE PEOPLE, GUYS N' DOLLS, WEST SIDE STORY (The Young Vic), TV; CHRISTMAS (Channel 4). Film; WHEN IN LONDON (Mad Hatter Productions).

Tracy Wiles – Linda

Tracy trained at The Royal Scottish Academy of Music & Drama. Theatre credits include; THE IMPORTANCE OF BEING EARNEST, ALICE'S ADVENTURES IN WONDERLAND (Dukes, Lancaster), CAPTAIN OF THE BIRDS (Young Vic Studio), BURDALANE (BAC), THE TRICK IS TO KEEP BREATHING (Tron Theatre, Glasgow, Royal Court, London and the Toronto World Stage Festival), TARTUFFE (Tron Theatre, Glasgow). TV includes; THE BILL, McCALLUM, A MUGS GAME. Film; SPEAK THE SPEECH: THE VOICE OF THE TEXT (Filmed in New York with the Voice Dept. of the RSC). Radio includes; Gracie Fields in GRACIE (Radio 4), Winner of the Carlton Hobbs BBC Radio Drama Award 1995.

Vicky Featherstone – Director

Trained at Manchester University and West Yorkshire Playhouse on the Regional Theatre Young Director Scheme. CRAZYHORSE is Vicky's first production for Paines Plough since her appointment as Artistic Director at the beginning of this year. Her most recent production was ANNA WEISS (Traverse Theatre, Edinburgh Festival '97), which won both Fringe First and Scotland on Sunday Critic's Awards. Other theatre includes; KVETCH, BRIGHTON ROCK (West Yorkshire Playhouse), TWO LIPS INDIF-FERENT RED (Bush Theatre), THE GLASS MENAGERIE, A CHRISTMAS CAROL, MY MOTHER SAID I NEVER SHOULD (Bolton Octagon), WOMEN PREFER . . . (Northern Stage). Other work includes; Script Development Executive for United Film and Television Productions, creating WHERE THE HEART IS and developing TOUCHING EVIL

Neil Warmington – Designer

Training: Fine art at Maidstone College of Art, Motley Theatre Design Course. Recent credits: COMEDIANS, ARSNIC AND OLD LACE (Lyceum, Edinburgh), LIFE IS A DREAM, FIDDLER ON THE ROOF (West Yorkshire Playhouse), MUCH ADO ABOUT NOTHING (Queen's Theatre, London), LIFE OF STUFF (Donmar), HENRY V (RSC), THE TEMPEST (Contact), WAITING FOR GODOT (Liverpool Everyman), CORIOLANUS (Tramway), ANGELS IN AMERICA (7:84/Traverse Theatre), DESIRE UNDER THE ELMS, JANE EYRE (Shared Experience/Young Vic), WOMEN LAUGHING (Watford Palace), PASSING PLACES (Traverse). Opera: TROILUS AND CRESSIDA (Opera North), OEDIPUS REX (Hartford, Connecticut). Awards include: TMA Award for Best Designer, Linbury Prize for Stage Design and the Alfred Munnings Florence prize for Painting.

Ian Scott – Lighting Designer

Trained at Mountview Theatre School. Recent projects include; TIMELESS (Suspect Culture, Edinburgh International Festival), INVISIBLE BULLETS (Blast Theory, Transeuropa 97), CALEDONIA DREAMING (7:84 Theatre Company). Ian is a regular member of the creative team at 7:84 and has lit, amongst others,

ANGELS IN AMERICA, THE GRAPES OF WRATH, THE LAMENT FOR ARTHUR CLEARY and WAR IN HEAVEN. Other work in the UK includes; WHAT THE BUTLER SAW (Graeae), FROGS (Royal National Theatre), THE HOUSE OF THE SPIRITS (Shaw Theatre), 20 MOVEMENTS (Scottish Chamber Orchestra – Mayfest), AIRPORT (Suspect Culture), STALINLAND (Citizens Theatre), HAPPY FAMILIES (Watford Palace) and UNIDENTIFIED HUMAN REMAINS (Traverse Theatre).

Mike Furness – Sound Designer

Mike was live mixing engineer for a number of West End shows including BEATLEMANIA, ANNIE, JESUS CHRIST SUPERSTAR, BUGSY MALONE, SONG AND DANCE, THE BOYFRIEND, THE HIRED MAN.
West End designs include ALLS WELL THAT ENDS WELL and AS YOU LIKE IT for the RSC at The Barbican. THE MANCHURIAN CANDIDATE (New Vic), ALL FOR NOTHING AT ALL (Tricycle), HOUSE OF THE SUN (Theatre Royal, Stratford East), WOMEN OF THE DUST (Bristol Old Vic), A YEARNING and A SHAFT OF SUNLIGHT (Birmingham Rep). As well as designing sound systems for live events world wide he also finds time to produce Talking Books.

Paines Plough

Artistic Director — Vicky Featherstone
Administrative Director — Belinda Hamilton
Literary Director — Mark Ravenhill
Literary Manager — Jessica Dromgoole
Administrator — Lucy Morrison
Writer in Residence (ACE funded) — Sarah Kane

Paines Plough, 4th Floor, 43 Aldwych, London WC2B 4DA
Tel. 0171 240 4533. *Fax:* 0171 240 4534
Email: paines.plough@dial.pipex.com

Tara Arts

Artistic Director — Jatinder Verma
Administrator — Matthew Jones
Centre Manager — Hitesh Chauhan
Project Co-ordinator — Sophie Robson
Dramaturg — Iqbal Husain

Tara Arts, 356 Garratt Lane, London SW18
Tel. 0181 333 4457. *Fax:* 0181 870 9540
Email: tara@tara-arts.com *Website:* http://www.tara-arts.com

CRAZYHORSE premiered at The New Vic Studio, Bristol Old Vic before embarking on a national tour to the following venues:

16-18 October	Watermans, London
23-25 October	Stephen Joseph Theatre, Scarborough
29 Oct – 1 Nov	Traverse Theatre, Edinburgh
4-22 November	BAC, London
27-29 November	Mercury Theatre, Colchester
2-4 December	Live Theatre, Newcastle

In spring 1998, Paines Plough will present SLEEPING AROUND – a mosaic of new voices, meshed in a game of theatrical Chinese whispers by Hilary Fannin, Stephen Greenhorn, Abi Morgan and Mark Ravenhill, first developed in association with The Royal National Theatre Studio.

In October 1998, Tara Arts will premiere EXODUS – the first of a millennium trilogy entitled JOURNEY TO THE WEST – the epic story of Asian migration to and transformation of England.

Parv Bancil
Crazyhorse

faber and faber
LONDON · BOSTON

First published in 1997
by Faber and Faber Limited
3 Queen Square London WC1N 3AU

Typeset by Country Setting, Woodchurch, Kent TN26 3TB
Printed in England by Intype London Ltd

A CIP record for this book
is available from the British Library

ISBN 0–571–19477–X

2 4 6 8 10 9 7 5 3 1

Characters

Jas

Ronnie

Mr Jutla

Nobby

Dead Woman

Act One

Night. A garage at the back of a house. Downstage is a window and double up-and-over doors. The walls of the garage are covered in pin-ups of nude women and cars. The place is well kitted out with an assortment of tools. In the middle of the floor is a pit, which is boarded up. A work bench and a chest of drawers are up against the wall stage right. A telephone and four wooden tea chests are up against the wall at stage left. Jas places a silver toaster on the workbench. The garage lights flicker and buzz for a moment. Jas freezes. Moment. He moves to the crates and takes out an old calendar from 1974: it is from an Indian shop and has a picture of a Sikh guru on it. Jas looks at it for a moment. He takes it over and places it on top of the calendar of a naked woman. Moment. He moves to the tea chests and empties one onto the floor. Amongst the various bits and pieces Jas finds an old prayer book and a dress. He picks these up and moves to the work bench. Jas smells the dress, then the book. Moment. He caresses the dress. Pause. The lights buzz, he drops the items onto the floor and runs to the corner of the garage. The lights buzz louder, the lights begin to flicker on and off. Jas cowers in the corner. The noise grows louder, the lights flicker like a strobe.

Jas Fuck off . . .

Lights and sound rise.

Please . . . Go . . . Just leave me!

The buzz becomes a deep hum. Jas covers his ears.

Leave me . . . Go! . . . Please . . .

The lights and sound fade out slowly. Jas remains in the same position.

Just leave me alone . . . Just leave . . .

Lights fade.

SCENE TWO

Garage. Afternoon. The toaster, crates and their contents are scattered around the garage. Ronnie stands by the window peering out into the next door neighbour's house. He wears an old but clean suit. Jas smokes a joint, sitting in the same position as the night before, and flicks through a porno mag. Both drink beer. Ronnie paces around. Moment. He turns to face Jas.

Ronnie So?

Jas No cash, no job.

Ronnie I need it tonight. I'll give you the cash later.

Jas Like last time?

Ronnie You blew the job!

Jas I waited an hour.

Ronnie Should've waited five more minutes.

Jas We arranged it.

Ronnie I got delayed.

Jas With the old bird.

Ronnie That's my business. You didn't have to dump the car. If you hadn't dumped it, they wouldn't have got your prints. Why didn't you wear gloves?

Jas I got three months.

Ronnie That's the way it crumbles. Take it on the chin. Three months is a holiday.

Jas I didn't grass.

Ronnie You think I would?

> *Beat.*

Jas You owe me money.

Ronnie Don't make me laugh. The car didn't arrive. We didn't get paid.

Jas I did my bit.

> *Pause.*

Ronnie I'm your mate, Jas. I need the favour.

> *Beat.*

Jas Cash up front.

Ronnie You want me to beg?

> *Moment.*

You only did six weeks.

> *Moment.*

I've had some serious cash problems.

> *Jas reads the mag. He doesn't look up.*

Gina's giving me grief. She suspects something. If I don't clear this up, she'll get wise and I'll be out the flat.

Jas Shouldn't cheat on the mother of your children, in' it.

Ronnie I was earning money, it was work! I did it for my kids so they can have clothes and eat food!

Jas Don't come at me with that . . .

Ronnie I need the job done.

Jas I've said my piece.

Ronnie What about the old days, Jas, me and you was like brothers. What happened?

Jas There ain't no problem, Ronnie, but I need money up front. You let me down once.

Ronnie I'm sorry. I really am.

Beat.

I've got woman trouble. You know what that's like. in' it.

Jas The worst.

Ronnie See, you understand.

Jas That's why I'm keeping away from them.

Ronnie Gina gives me shit when I walk through that door. No matter what time of night. I wanted to tell her I was screwing an old bird for money but she wouldn't have understood. So I had to take all this shit, when all I was doin' was workin' for her. But I blew up last night. She gave me ear ache so I pinned her up and hung her on a coat hook.

Beat.

I had to, man. She was gettin' violent. So I said to her, I said, 'Listen 'ere woman, who's the man of the house? I go out every day to earn money. I make sure the rent is paid. I make sure the kids have enough food.' And she still complains. She says I ain't home enough. I said if

I was at home, we'd have no money. She said, 'I don' care about money.'

Jas We had it good then.

Ronnie Unlimited pussy on tap. They all hung around the guys who had money, all those old men, and what did they used to say?

Jas (*mimics a bimbo*) 'Ooh, I'm not interested in money – as long as the guy's got a nice personality.' Bollocks.

Ronnie If they knew we was gettin' the night bus home . . .

Both Nah, mate.

Ronnie Cash is what they want. Once they've got you, that's it. Take Gina. When I first met that girl, I was so stiff I couldn't walk. She was dressed to kill, nice legs, nice hair . . . She was fit, now she looks like a sack of kak.

Jas Women go like that after they have kids.

Ronnie Then she wonders why I sleep around.

Jas Get rid of her then.

Ronnie turns and peers out of the window. Pause.

Ronnie Look – look! The dirty bastard's at it again, look, see.

Jas ignores Ronnie.

Come on Jas, you're missing the action . . . It's him, the bloke with the turban. He's just standing there. I think she's going to whip the man to rass!

Moment.

Eh? Where she gone now? I bet she's givin' 'im 'ead. I betcha. Come see, Jas. Get the real live action, not magazine picture.

Jas You're full of shit, Ronnie.

Ronnie I don't think so, man. Who's the one with the ideas and connections. Not you methinks. Not any more.

Ronnie Come on, Jas. Look at you wasting away like this. It should be like it was in the old days. We used to take Porsches and Cosworths and strip them down in one night.

Jas So.

Beat. Ronnie kicks the toaster.

Ronnie Is this what you do for money these days, petty burglaries?

Jas It was a good plan. It got fucked up.

Ronnie It wouldn't have if you had brought me in.

Jas It was short notice.

Ronnie I saw Nobby on the way home last night. He told me the score.

Jas I didn't have time to tell you.

Ronnie That's an insult. I would've told you.

Jas Don't get all up on me. You've done things without tellin' me.

Ronnie That's fair enough. We need to get our money from whatever means, but Nobby's an arsehole. I'm your mate, see, I don't mind you trying to do a crafty one but I want it to be worth your while when you do it. The Porsche will be worth your while. We were a good team. Don't let this prison shit fuck that up. You think I don't feel bad about what happened?

Beat.

I'll never forget what you did for me. This is why I'm offering you this chance.

Jas Chance?

Ronnie One Porsche. It might lead to other work. I could set you up in a place and we could do this thing full time. Look at all the tools you have.

Jas They're my Dad's.

Ronnie When's the last time 'im pick up a spanner?

Jas Still his.

Ronnie What's 'appened to you, man?

Jas It's alright for you to be all bloody happy but that's 'cos you ain't done bird.

Ronnie searches around the garage.

Ronnie Shit! Wood – gimme wood!

Jas points to the broom. Ronnie seizes it with both hands.

Touch wood I never will.

Jas Might teach you a lesson.

Ronnie Don't say those things. It can cause you bad Karma. You should know that Indian boy.

Jas Load of bollocks.

Ronnie Wha? It's your culture. Ya na know nuthin? You should embrace it with pride.

Jas You're freaked out, Ronnie.

Ronnie No way. You ever hear of them voodoo people in Jamaica? There's some bad shit going on there and it works.

Jas Yea, right.

Ronnie My mother told me an' me mother don't lie. She's seen the dead coming back to life. Things happen y'know. Don't laugh at that shit.

Jas What you scared of? You don't even know what touchin' wood does.

Ronnie She told me that there's these doppis walking all around us. They say these people died before their time or were murdered and they don't know they're dead. If you know voodoo, you can capture the spirits and marry them to a dead body and bring it to life. Although it's a different body, they say the zombie can fool loved ones. They look into its eyes and they see the person who died.

Jas You wanna get together with the old man. I think this Rasta grass has taken its effect on you, mate.

Ronnie Your old man would cut my throat if he ever saw me here.

Jas Can't blame him.

Ronnie I'm askin' for a favour.

Jas I got no time for charity any more.

Pause.

Ronnie Charity? I should bust your 'ead! Look at you, man. You live like that Stig in the dump bloke. Look at the state of this place. This shows your state of mind.

Jas Money talks.

Ronnie You Indian man is devious. This is the manipulation coming into effect. You want more money, in' it?

Jas Sorry, Ronnie. I can't do it.

Ronnie Right. Some mate you turned out to be.

Jas Get it yourself.

Ronnie They know me down that street. Just go there and take the car.

Jas flicks through the magazine.

Ronnie You're lucky it's your birthday today, otherwise I wouldn't be so lenient.

Moment.

Alright, fuck you then! I'll see Jimmy Bains. He'll sort me out.

Ronnie heads for the door. He waits for Jas to change his mind. Jas ignores him.

Ronnie Jimmy's a good man . . . He's doing good trade. He doesn't need the money, Jas. Look. I don't mean to be out of order, but your Dad don't give a fuck about you. He's kicking you out.

Jas I don't wanna take the piss.

Beat.

Ronnie It ain't the money is it?

Beat.

Jas If the Police find any illegal stuff going on, they'll take his business.

Ronnie It's dead anyway.

Jas That's his worry. I'm not gonna kill it any more.

Ronnie I won't forget this.

Pause. Ronnie leaves.

Moment. The lights flicker and buzz. Jas seems to fall into a trance. He gets up from his corner and moves to the crates. He moves them from the pit, then searches around for a crowbar. The lights flicker faster, the buzz grows louder. He finds it. Jas begins to prise open one of the boards over the pit. He finds it difficult but manages it eventually. The stench is overpowering, he moves away to take air. He falls out of the trance state, and realises his whereabouts.

Mr Jutla (*offstage*) Jasbir! Where's my ticket?

The lights settle. The buzz disappers. Jas immediately replaces the board over the pit and puts the crates back on top. Mr Jutla enters. Moment.

I haven't got time for all this shit today. Where is it?

Jas Somewhere.

Mr Jutla Somewhere? What good is that to me? I can't take it out without the ticket.

Mr Jutla notices the crates. He moves to them.

I'll pick up the suit on my way to Jimmy Bains'. He's got a lot of work on. I'm sure he'll put some our way.

Mr Jutla takes a black dress from a crate. He holds it for a moment, then carefully folds it and places it back in the crate.

Get rid of it.

Jas I'll do it later.

Mr Jutla You always say that and nothing gets done.

Jas I work.

Mr Jutla That's why we have no business.

Jas I've been here.

Mr Jutla People complained.

Jas Not my fault.

Mr Jutla Whose fault is it then?

Jas I'm doin' my job. They all get favours outta you, they take the piss and I don't let them.

Mr Jutla It's the way business works. You give and take a little. Why charge to fix a door handle when the customer is paying you for an engine rebuild?

Jas It's extra work.

Mr Jutla It's part of the game. You have to learn how to play it.

Jas I work out an hourly rate.

Mr Jutla It takes you twice as long doing it.

Jas That's the pace I work at, take it or leave it.

Mr Jutla Looks like the customers have made their decision.

Jas Not my fault. It's not me who's been on holiday with a married woman.

Mr Jutla She's a widow.

Jas By her own doing, I heard. The last bloke's hardly cold.

Mr Jutla Don't ever talk like that in front of me ever again you little shit.

Jas lights a cigarette. Mr Jutla moves to him and takes it from his mouth, throws it on the floor and stamps on it.

There's petrol in here.

Jas It's her second husband that's died, everyone knows that.

Mr Jutla That's my problem. Now, I want you to get her car fixed and dropped off at the pub.

Jas Is she paying for it?

Mr Jutla You have no rights here. You lost them after your little holiday!

Mr Jutla notices the calendar. He takes it down. Underneath is a calendar of a nude woman.

Jas That's mine.

Mr Jutla I said get rid of all of it.

Jutla puts the calendar into a crate.

Jas Everyone knows she's a free-loader.

Mr Jutla Shut up, idiot.

Jas Two houses she got outta her two dead husbands. Hope you're not gonna let her get the third.

Mr Jutla Have you found a place to live yet?

Jas I've looked.

Mr Jutla Then look harder. I don't want a car thief here.

Jas It was a mistake. You're being too hard.

Mr Jutla That's the way life goes my boy, not everything comes easy.

Jutla looks around at the mess on the floor.

Look at the state of this place.

Jas I was going to clean it.

Jutla picks up a beer can.

Mr Jutla Haven't your so called friends got anything else to do with their lives? Bloody drunks.

Jas They're not drunks,

Mr Jutla I know drunks when I see them. Who do you think I spend most of my time with down the pub? Drunks.

Jutla throws the can on the floor. He picks up the toaster.

Where did you get this from?

Jas Nobby left it. We were trying to make toast.

Mr Jutla Give that idiot a call. I want him to finish that wall today. It's taken him a week already. I'm not paying him by the hour so tell him to get a move on or I'll deduct money from his fee.

Jas You tell him.

Mr Jutla You've got a big mouth on you. Don't you have any respect for anybody?

Jas Who?

Mr Jutla Sons should respect their fathers.

Jas Just like that?

Mr Jutla Yes.

Beat. Mr Jutla looks around the garage for his ticket.

Where the bloody hell did you put it?

Jas It's my birthday today.

Beat.

I'm twenty-three.

Mr Jutla Look in your pockets.

Jas We're thinking of having a drink to celebrate tonight.

Mr Jutla I had that suit hand made in Savile Row.

Jas Fancy a drink with us?

Mr Jutla Do what you bloody well want. I need my suit.

Jas This one's alright.

Mr Jutla I want the blue one.

Jas You wear that on special occasions. Going out to dinner with a barmaid doesn't sound very special to me.

Mr Jutla It is for me.

Jutla hands Jas the broom.

Clear this up and find it.

Jas Wear this one, Dad.

Mr Jutla Once you've done it, I want her car fixed and dropped off.

Jas She can get a bus.

Mr Jutla It's dangerous for her to get home alone at that time of night. Anything can happened to a woman on her own in that park. I don't like her crossing it.

Jas I'm taking a day off.

Moment.

Mr Jutla You can't just take time off. You may not be in prison, but don't think you've gotten away with it! I'll sort you out once and for all.

Pause.

I have to see Jimmy.

Jas To beg.

Mr Jutla To ask a favour.

Jas To grovel.

Mr Jutla Your little holiday fucked up this business.

Jas Don't blame me . . .

Mr Jutla Nobody wants to bring their car to a thief's garage!

Jas He didn't call, he didn't ask for help.

Mr Jutla No, but . . .

Jas Then he doesn't need it.

Mr Jutla I've just about had enough of your . . .

Jas Really?

Mr Jutla Cocky shit.

Jas She's after your money, Dad.

Mr Jutla What money? We don't have any money.

Moment.

Jas We've got the house. That's all we've got.

Mr Jutla Don't be ridiculous.

Jas I'm tellin' you . . .

Mr Jutla raises his hand to Jas. Moment.

Mr Jutla How dare you talk to me like that. I built up this business from nothing, with pure hard work and determination. What have you ever had to do in your life.

Jas At least I don't have to beg.

Jas I'm trying to save our business. Jimmy's an old friend, a friend who I helped when he was starting out. I have to ask a man who looks up to me like an older brother for help. How do you think that makes me feel? I'm doing it so we can eat.

Jas Not my fault. I haven't been on holiday with the slag and her kid.

Mr Jutla She's good to me.

Jas She's a slag.

Mr Jutla Enough.

Jas That's why you want me to get rid of these.

Mr Jutla Shut up.

Jas I'm not stupid. You can't even wish me a happy birthday, can you. Say it.

Moment.

Why can't you say it to me?

Jutla exits. Moment. Jas moves to the crates and takes out the dress, a prayer book and calendar. He hangs it over the nude picture. Jas steps back and admires it. He then picks up the dress and caresses it gently. He puts it down. Moment. Jas takes the crowbar and begins to prise off the boards on the pit.

Lights fade.

SCENE THREE

Garage. The lights flicker and buzz. The boards have been removed from the pit, they are stacked up against the wall. Jas takes the last of the crates and puts it in the pit. Nobby watches from the door. Jas replaces the planks. The lights and buzz disappear. Jas notices Nobby.

Nobby What're you burying?

Jas What?

Nobby Why did you bury the crates in the pit? We're supposed to throw them away.

Jas What you talking about, Nobby?

Nobby You're windin' me up again in' it? You're trying to freak me out again, in' it? But it ain't gonna work, Rasta.

Jas is confused.

Jas Ain't you got work to do?

Nobby It's my break.

Jas You've only been in half n' hour.

Nobby It's too hot out there. Man's got to save energy or he'll die working in the field for the man.

Moment. Nobby moves to the window. He gestures Jas to join him.

He's there again.

Jas moves to the window.

Jas Can you see anything?

Nobby He's just standing there.

Jas Is she there?

Nobby He's got a big grin on his face. I bet she's sucking his cock. I bet he's got his pants down and she's whipping his arse with a leather whip.

Jas Or maybe there's more than one of them. He could be standing there while all of them are sitting on a sofa and he's choosing which one he wants.

Nobby He's probably been through most of them and he wants something different.

Jas Something new.

Pause.

She must be white.

Nobby Why?

Jas 'Cos that's what he wants. I bet he's got a wife at home and she must be Indian . . .

Nobby You're generalising, man.

Jas Shut up, Nobby. He's got a turban, in' it. So he's gone to old slag's house to get something different.

Nobby That makes sense. I wish I had a brain like yours.

Both watch in silence. Moment.

Both Bollocks!

Nobby They always close the curtains at the good bit.

Beat.

How much sand and cement do I mix up?

Jas You're the bricklayer.

Nobby It's five parts sand to one part cement for something, and three parts sand to one part cement for something else. I just don't know which one it is.

Jas Three parts for walls and five for driveways.

Nobby You sure?

Jas Yeah.

Moment. Nobby watches Jas putting the planks back.

Nobby Gonna use the pit?

Pause.

Nobby Makes working underneath easier. But you've gotta clean it out first. That smells bad, man. It smells putrid. Like rotting flesh in the pit of Hell. Thousands of bodies have been buried in there over the years, all rotting and becoming one.

Moment.

Jas Don't tell the old man I opened it.

Nobby Hiding something special.

Jas Just old stuff I wanna keep.

Nobby You said it was junk.

Jas I changed my mind.

Nobby When.

Jas Now . . . I suppose.

Nobby You're hidin' somethin' else, in' it? Something secret.

Jas No.

Nobby Then you're going insane. I've seen that weird look in your eye. You can tell it all from the eye, I learnt that in India, I did. You had that black look in your eye, a dark far away kind of thing, it was as if you were really focused . . .

Jas spots the toaster.

Jas You always fuck things up. I tell you to do something small and you mess it up.

Nobby That's not fair. When was the last time?

Jas Three o'clock this morning.

Nobby It was a mistake. We all make them.

Jas What a waste of time. All I asked you to do was pick up the box.

Nobby It was dark, I couldn't tell.

Jas Two weeks I spent checkin' that place over.

Nobby I was just following orders. You said pick up the box, so I did.

Jas The jewellery box, not the toaster.

Nobby It was dark.

Jas How many jewellery boxes have a lead and a plug on them? Imagine getting done for nicking a toaster.

Moment.

Nobby Aggravated burglary's a serious offence. We shouldn't have hit him. We could get a couple of years for that.

Jas Why'd you tell Ronnie? He's gonna tell everyone! I'll never be able to face anyone again. There was a least four grands' worth of gold in that box. The old man bought it for his daughter's wedding.

Moment.

Nobby Five parts sand for walls was it?

Jas Three.

Nobby Oh yeah.

Nobby turns to exit. He stops.

I'm sorry, Jas, I didn't mean to do it . . . I always fuck things up, don't I?

Beat.

I'll just go and fix the wall . . .

24

Jas Have your break.

Nobby I'm alright.

Jas Look, I just wanted to say thanks.

Nobby For what?

Jas When you came to visit me in the nick.

Nobby Don't mention that. That's what mates are for.

Jas I know. I just wanted you to know. That gear helped me get through.

Nobby moves to the cupboard and looks through it. He finds a half loaf of bread. He sniffs it.

Nobby Had breakfast?

Jas No.

Nobby Fancy some toast?

Jas gives Nobby a dirty look. Nobby plugs in the toaster.

Reckon the bread's alright?

Nobby throws it to Jas. Jas checks it.

Jas There's some blue mouldy stuff on it.

Jas scrapes off the fungus. He sniffs the bread.

That'll do.

Nobby That's it, positive thinking, that's the way forward.

Nobby pops the bread into the toaster. Both watch and wait. Moment. Jas checks the socket. Pause. He checks the lead. Long pause. Silence.

I think it's broken.

Jas Bloody typical. Hardly gonna get us on *Crimewatch*, is it? Two hardened toaster thieves on the rampage. Police warn the public not to approach them because they are likely to kick the living shit outta you to obtain your broken kitchen appliances! You fuckin' idiot, Nobby!

Nobby Don't put me on that trip, man. I was just followin' orders.

Nobby moves to the cupboard. He takes out two unhealthy looking potatoes and puts them into a pan. He fills the pan with water and lights the gas burner. He places the pan onto it.

Why won't he let you use the kitchen?

Jas Overstayed my welcome. I'm lucky he lets me sleep in here.

Nobby Got that Fiesta to fix, then?

Jas Bollocks, it's for her, in' it. I'm not fixing his woman's car. Runs around like a slave after her.

Nobby He's in love, in' it.

Jas She's using him and he can't see it.

Nobby takes a spliff from his pocket. He hands it to Jas.

Nobby Don't freak out. I know you don't like celebrating it, but I thought you might like a smoke.

Jas takes the spliff.

Just save me some, in' it.

Jas lights it.

(*mimics Mr Jutla*) There's petrol in here!

Jas smiles.

26

I'm hungry. We need some meat. We need to get strong, 'cos I believe man need meat to live. Chicken with rice and peas, yes, me could mash that up right now, Rasta.

Jas Go to the shop, then.

Nobby Me have no dollar.

Jas Tough.

Nobby You must have some decent food inside. The man has no soul.

Moment

Lend us a fiver.

Jas Ain't got any.

Nobby A tenner then.

Jas Idiot.

Nobby That was a joke. Get it? A tenner's more than a fiver.

Jas Is it really.

Nobby laughs. He repeatedly flicks his wrists and slaps his forefinger against the middle finger.

Nobby Of course it is. You're a bit thick sometimes ain't ya. Rass clat . . . Bumba clat!

Nobby is in hysterics.

Jas Your girlfriend come back did she?

Silence. Moment.

Nobby Why, you seen her?

Jas Might 'ave.

Nobby Did you?

Jas She was in town with some suit.

Nobby Cunt!

Jas At least you know.

Nobby She told me she needed space.

Jas Women are born liars.

Nobby She said she wanted to be on her own. I asked if there was another bloke. I'll kill her.

Jas Would you?

Nobby Bitch.

Jas Would you?

Nobby What?

Jas If she was here right now, would you kill her?

Nobby I want her back.

Jas After she's run off with a suit?

Nobby Life's worse without her. Every day's shit.

Jas All I ever saw you do was ruc. You said you wanted to break it off.

Nobby I did. But I don't now.

Jas It's happened, though.

Nobby Life's a cunt. Can't live with 'em . . .

Jas Yeah, I know.

> *Moment. Both stare into space. Silence. Enter Ronnie, he looks flustered. Ronnie looks over to Jas. Moment. Jas turns away. Nobby moves to greet Ronnie with hand outstretched.*

Nobby Alright, dread. How's it going, ya ras clat. How's the picknee's and the Missis? She back at yard is she? Bet she's makin you all that yam and rice n' peas in' it?

Ronnie moves to Jas. Nobby is left with hand outstretched.

Ronnie So what y' sayin', Jas?

Jas Thought you were going to Jimmy's.

Ronnie Man's a fool. He's gettin' too big headed for his own good. Don't remember those that've done him favours. Now he's got money, he don't wanna know. People gettin' too up on themselves lately, it's hard to find genuine 'friends' any more.

Nobby What's the problem, dread?

Ronnie Come on, Jas, time's running out.

Jas Can't do it, mate.

Ronnie Small. You guys are too small.

Jas Take it somewhere else.

Ronnie lights the cigarette and paces the garage.

Ronnie What planet are you on?

Ronnie flicks ash on the floor.

Nobby Careful, there's petrol in here.

Ronnie Petrol? You're lucky I don't torch the whole fuckin' garage. Comprehend this. Y'see, I'm on the moon. I can see everything. And you two – you're stuck on the Earth and I can see all around you. Everything. The sun, the stars . . .

Nobby I dig what you're sayin', brov. We can see all that from here too, Rasta.

Ronnie Yea, from down here, not from the moon. I'm on the moon. From here the sun looks different – it's a ball of fire. From Earth it's a hazy smudge. I can see what's in front of you and behind you. I can see it all from the moon.

Silence. Nobby looks to Jas for an explanation.

Jas I'll be fucked if I know what he's on about.

Ronnie You have to be here to see it. You have to be where I am.

Nobby moves and stands on Ronnie's toes. Moment. Ronnie slaps Nobby across the head.

Move, ya sap!

Nobby I just wanted to see.

Ronnie I mean it metaphorically.

Ronnie notices the potatoes.

Ronnie Potatoes? What 'appened to all that curry n' ting you people eat?

Ronnie takes out his wallet. He hands Nobby a twenty pound note.

Dogs eat better than you. Nobby, go to the shop and get some man food, chicken and chips. Eat like men. Get some beers.

Jas Go on, Nobby.

Nobby D'you want chilli sauce?

Jas Go!

Nobby kisses his lips. He exits. Moment.

Ronnie Why'd you put up with 'im? The man's a fool.

Jas He's alright.

Pause.

Ronnie I saw your old man at Jimmy's.

Jas So.

Ronnie Seemed pretty desperate for work.

Jas He is.

Ronnie That's a shame. It's bad to see how things turn out for some people, especially two old friends that go way back. Started out together, didn't they?

Pause.

I'd never do that to an old friend, y'see, that's what friends are for. That's why we have them, that's why friendships last longer than most marriages. Friends help each other out. They don't make demands. I always remember your old man as being this guy who ran things around here. No one fucked with him or his crew. But there he was, sitting in this office like some little kid outside the headmaster's door. That's when I saw a big man look small. And who made him look like that, his best friend.

Jas So, what's the point. He went to beg for overload work from Jimmy's and didn't get it. You think I didn't know that? My old man tells me everything.

Ronnie You sure 'bout that, rude boy?

Jas Everything.

Ronnie I heard him tellin' Jimmy stuff about that woman of his, Linda. He's taking her out tonight.

Jas Big deal.

Ronnie Did you pick up his suit? His special suit.

Jas I lost the ticket.

Ronnie He was blowing steam at Jimmy's.

Jas I told him to wear the other one, what's his problem.

Ronnie He wanted his blue one. He said it was tailor made at Savile Row.

Jas So.

Ronnie So, he said a few other things n' all.

Jas I don't really give a fuck 'bout where he takes that woman. She's just another bird that he's spending time with.

Ronnie Didn't sound like that to me.

Jas What did it sound like?

Ronnie Just what I heard.

Moment.

Ronnie picks up the calendar and the dress.

Funny how he's clearin' out your Mum's stuff, in' it?

Jas No. It's time for us to move on. Forget.

Ronnie Why today?

Jas It's my birthday.

Beat.

Ronnie Add it up, Jas. The suit? The clear out? Him kicking you out.

Jas What you sayin', Ronnie?

Ronnie Forget it. This sort of stuff should only be shared amongst friends.

Jas I'm your mate.

Ronnie I thought you were too, but now it seems you've changed your mind.

Jas I am your mate.

Ronnie Don't know how to say this exactly but, Jas, I think your old man's lying to you. Y'see, he was tellin' Jimmy that his dinner with Linda was special and that's why he needed the suit, the clear out and you leaving home. He's gonna ask her to marry him and move into the house.

Pause.

Jas Bollocks!

Ronnie He wants that son of hers in too, as soon as you go.

Jas I don't believe you.

Ronnie It's what he said.

Jas Why you sayin' this Ronnie? Just 'cos I don't wanna do that car for you . . . This is low. I thought you were a mate.

Ronnie I am.

Enter Jutla. He notices Ronnie straight away. Beat.

Mr Jutla Did you find it?

Jas Not yet.

Mr Jutla Then bloody well look for it. I'm running late.

Jutla notices the calendar. He looks around for the crates. He can't see them. He moves to the calendar.

I said get rid of it all. This place is a bloody circus.

Ronnie Hello, Mr. Jutla, how'd your meeting go at Jimmy's?

33

Beat.

Mr Jutla None of your business.

Ronnie Just making conversation.

Mr Jutla You never make conversation, Ronnie. There's always a hidden agenda with you.

Ronnie If you say so.

Mr Jutla Where's that idiot? He's left the cement in the sun and it's dried up.

Ronnie He went to get some chicken.

Mr Jutla notices the potatoes.

Mr Jutla What's this muck?

Jas My dinner.

Mr Jutla Bloody savages. Tell that idiot that I'm taking money off his wages to replace the cement he's wasted.

Jutla takes the calendar down to reveal the nude picture.

I want him to finish that wall today. He's been on it a week, it's a day's work.

Jas It's cheap.

Mr Jutla That's no excuse. Have you fixed the car yet?

Jas I'll do it.

Mr Jutla I don't want her to catch a bus tonight.

Jas Never does anyway from what I hear.

Mr Jutla Shut it and fix the car you idiot.

Jas Going somewhere important?

Mr Jutla You know where I'm going.

Jas Indian?

Mr Jutla No . . . I thought I'd try the Italian on Duke Street.

Jas Expensive.

Mr Jutla Makes a change.

Jas Really.

Moment.

Mr Jutla What's your point?

Jas Nothing. I didn't mean anything.

Mr Jutla It's always nothing. You talk a lot and say nothing. That's the sign of a complete idiot.

Jas I'm sorry I haven't got Linda's son's brains. Sorry I didn't go to a grammar school. But you couldn't give me the time of day, could you?

Mr Jutla Stop feeling sorry for yourself.

Jas Why d'you want the blue suit?

Jutla looks over to Ronnie. Ronnie looks to the floor.

Mr Jutla That's my affair.

Jas Your special suit. Your hand made suit from Savile Row.

Mr Jutla I want to look smart.

Jas Why did we clear out Mum's things?

Mr Jutla I'm in a rush.

Jutla moves to the door.

Jas You're going to ask her to marry you, aren't you?

Pause.

What about Mum?

Jutla turns to face Jas.

Mr Jutla She's dead.

Jas She's still here.

Mr Jutla You're insane.

Jas She comes here . . . Sometimes . . .

Mr Jutla You're twenty-three now. Act like a man, not a boy!

Jas You can't do this to her.

Mr Jutla It's not about her, it's about you.

Moment. Jutla exits. Long pause.

Ronnie Sorry Jas . . .

Moment.

Jimmy turned him down. Wouldn't give the old man any work. He said he didn't trust him.

Pause. Jas takes a blue ticket from his pocket. He takes a lighter and burns it. Ronnie takes a car key from his pocket, he offers it to Jas. Jas takes it. Ronnie smiles.

Lights fade.

Act Two

SCENE ONE

Night. The lights in the garage are switched off. Only the strong moonlight illuminates the space. Nobby and Ronnie are on stage. Only their silhouettes can be seen. Nobby lights a cigarette, he then lights Ronnie's cigarette.

Ronnie You shouldn't wear that. Ain't you got no respect for yourself?

Nobby It's only a laugh, in' it. He'll have a right laugh when he gets back.

Ronnie You're sick in the head.

Nobby You got no sense of humour. You're boring.

Ronnie I'm putting up with this stupid idea of yours, in' it.

Nobby That's 'cos it's a good one.

Ronnie kisses his teeth.

How'd you do that, brov?

Ronnie Stupid boy.

Moment. Nobby tries to kiss his teeth, it sounds like air escaping from a balloon. Pause. He tries again. Moment.

Nobby You got the candles?

Ronnie I could only get this one.

Nobby One?

Ronnie It's late, in' it.

Nobby The man's twenty-three.

Ronnie Don't worry, it's the thought that counts.

Nobby Suppose so.

Ronnie takes a long drag from his cigarette. Moment.

Ronnie He'll freak.

Nobby Have faith, bred.

Beat.

Ronnie I had to tell him 'bout Linda. You know that don't you? I didn't say it so he'd go get the car or anything. You know that.

Nobby Things have to be said. Sometimes you've got to face the music.

Ronnie Jutla's bang out of order.

Nobby The man's always been sly. It's in the eyes. He's got dodgy eyes. They are the windows to our souls. Look in my eyes, can you see? They give it all away. Never trust a person who never looks you in the eye. Learnt that in India, I did.

Moment.

Can you see my soul?

Ronnie No.

Nobby Let me look in your eyes. I bet I can see your soul.

Ronnie Get off! The only 'sole' you're likely to see is the one on the bottom of my shoe when I kick your arse.

Nobby You wanna get out to India. They love us black guys out there.

Pause.

Ronnie But you ain't black.

Nobby What you talkin' about, Rasta? Don't be racist. I hate racists. It ain't about colour, black comes from within. I ain't being funny, Ronnie. But I think I'm blacker than you.

Ronnie Shut up fool. Go get your hair cut! Dreads don't suit white boys. You think just 'cos you locks your hair and smoke ganja that you can be anything you want. Well, it don't work. One minute you're a skinhead and the next this Indian . . . Rasta . . . you're a lost case.

Nobby I've changed.

Ronnie I preferred the old you. At least I knew who you were.

Nobby I know who I am, that's what's important.

Pause.

Ronnie Where is he?

Nobby He'll be alright.

Ronnie Half an hour late already.

Nobby His old man's gonna kill him. He didn't take the Fiesta to Linda.

Ronnie This is more important.

Nobby What if he got caught again?

Ronnie desperately searches the room for the broom. He finds it.

Ronnie Grab this!

Nobby Me no believe in superstition n' all that.

Ronnie grabs Nobby's hand. He forces him to touch the broomstick.

Ronnie We don't wanna encourage bad luck.

Ronnie sniffs the air.

What's that smell?

Nobby What's it smell of?

Ronnie If I knew that. I wouldn't ask, in' it.

Nobby Can't smell nuthin'.

Ronnie Smells like somethin' rotting. It's like shit.

Moment.

It's your head, man.

Nobby Shut up.

Ronnie When's the last time you washed that stuff on your head?

Nobby Can't remember.

Ronnie Get it sorted. That's disgusting!

Nobby It's the smell of nature. It's beautiful. Hair cleans itself.

Ronnie Clean? Get it cut, you dirty tramp. Oh shit, that smell vile.

Nobby Don't wanna get it cut. I went to the hairdresser's 'bout two and a half years ago. It's the last time I had a crop. I went there with Jas, we had blade ones. The man took our souls with our hair, and we paid him to do it. Nah, bred. Your hair makes you strong like Samson and Delilah. Once I realised that, the whole world made sense. Hairdressers work for the government. When they take your hair, they take your free will. Why d'you think all the Babylon and army man has short hair? Why d'you think all the man who work in the city like robots have short hair? Think about it. Once you get a job in the city, they ask you to cut your hair.

Ronnie Don't talk crap.

Nobby Look at you. Now you've got your hair cut, all you wanna do is make money and ting.

Ronnie You come out with the most stupidness.

Nobby Okay, alright . . . What if I did want to get my hair cut and I didn't know about the conspiracy. There's other reasons not to go, much simpler ones.

Ronnie Like?

Nobby . . . It's hassle in' it.

Ronnie It's not hassle. Not everything in life's a party, is it?

Nobby Don't make me laugh. Not hassle? Where do you live, Rasta? I mean, where do you start, which one d'you go to? It does your head in.

Ronnie There's loads.

Nobby What if they fuck it up, though?

Ronnie Eh?

Nobby If I did get it cut, and I wanted it short. They could really mess it up.

Ronnie Get a crop.

Nobby Nah, I wouldn't get it that short. What would I say to the hairdresser?

Ronnie Say you want a short haircut, a short back n' sides.

Nobby He might end up giving me a side parting and I'd end up looking stupid.

Ronnie Can't look more stupid than you do now, believe me, dread.

Nobby Would they wash it?

Ronnie Comes out better.

Moment.

Nobby I think I'll leave it long.

Moment.

Once you get there, you have to wait around. That's when I start freaking out. All these people just sitting there looking tired, they all like they wanna die. Some look like their wives have left them and their kids don't care any more. 'What's life all about,' they think to themselves as they sit there. 'What's it all for?' Then they die. Hairdressers freak me out.

Moment.

Ronnie I don't know where you got your hair cut, but I'll make sure I keep away from there.

A sports car pulls up outside.

Nobby Got the lighter?

Ronnie lights the candle. Nobby takes a cake out of a box. Ronnie places the candle in the centre of the cake. Both wait. Moment. Jas enters. He turns the lights on. Nobby is wearing the dress over his clothes. Both Ronnie and Nobby wear paper party hats. Ronnie holds the cake.

Ronnie and **Nobby** Surprise!

*Jas stands centre stage with Linda's dead body in his
arms. Her body has some blood on it. All freeze.*

*Long pause. Jas gently lays the body down onto the
garage floor. Beat. He looks across at Nobby for the
first time since he walked in. Beat.*

*Jas hurls himself at Nobby, he tries to pull his dress
off. The cake is pushed into Ronnie's face. Jas tears at
the dress. He begins to punch Nobby violently. Ronnie
stares at the body, he slowly scrapes the cake off his
face.*

Nobby It's a joke, man!

Ronnie What happened?

*Nobby tries to take the dress off. Jas punches him on
the nose. Nobby's nose bleeds. The lights buzz and
flicker. Jas moves away from Nobby. Ronnie cleans
the cake from his face.*

Nobby It was a joke . . .

Pause.

We wanted you to be happy, that's all.

Ronnie What happened . . .

Nobby feels the blood on his face.

Nobby I think it's broken.

*Jas picks up the dress. He holds it against him. Nobby
takes a packet of cigarettes from his jeans. He offers
one to Jas. Jas is in shock. Beat. He scrapes up the
cake off the floor and puts it back onto the cake tray.*

Ronnie What happened, Jas?

*Beat. Nobby lights up. The telephone rings. It rings
for a long time.*

What happened?

The telephone rings twice more. It stops. Long pause. Ronnie grabs Jas by the collar and shakes him violently. Jas does not retaliate, he stares at the body in shock.

Why didn't you just come home . . . You cunt.

Nobby Is she dead?

Jas She just . . . I didn't mean . . . I swear I pressed the brake . . . It was an accident.

Ronnie But my car . . . I'll lose five grand!

Moment.

Nobby There's a dead woman here.

Ronnie I didn't kill her.

Jas It was an accident, I swear it was.

The telephone rings. Ronnie moves to it.

Jas Don't.

Ronnie I gave you the keys. All you had to do was drive the fucker home.

Nobby Shut up for fuck's sake! We need to think . . .

Jas I don't know why I went there.

Ronnie Don't tell me you didn't know why you went there! This is your old man's woman!

Jas I went to pick her up . . . I just felt bad about her walking through that park on her own . . .

Ronnie So you killed her!

Beat.

He killed her.

Beat

We're in a murder situation here. This isn't happening.
I'll wake up in a minute . . . I'll wake up.

Jas I didn't kill her!

Ronnie Then who did?

Jas I just went there to . . . I went there . . .

Ronnie To kill her.

Jas NO!

Nobby Jas, this doesn't look good, y'know what I mean.

Jas I swear she stepped out in front of me.

Nobby Where?

Jas In the park.

Ronnie The park? That's way out from where you was
supposed to go . . .

Nobby The park's not on your way home, dread.

Ronnie You fuckin' . . .

Jas I saw her walking. I wanted to slow down to give
her a lift but I saw . . . I saw something that . . . And she
was there. I swear I pressed the brake . . .

Ronnie You fucked it all up now!

Jas I kept thinking, that's my old man's woman. She the
person he wants to marry and bring into my Mum's
house.

Beat.

Nobby So you did it!

Jas No . . . I don't know. That's what I was thinking at
the time but I . . . I didn't mean to do it.

45

Ronnie So you did it.

Jas I don't know how.

Ronnie You have to know! How can you not know?

Jas I can't explain . . . I know I did it, but I didn't mean to.

Ronnie Why were you there? You didn't have to go there.

Jas Nobby. You believe me don't you?

Nobby We have to get rid of the body, Jas.

Jas If I go to the Police. They might believe me.

Ronnie I don't believe you, man. You think they will?

Beat.

We've got to get rid of the car, Ronnie.

Beat. Jas looks around the garage. Jas finds the electric saw.

Jas We'll get rid of the car, and then her . . .

Ronnie Hold on . . .

Jas Bring it in, Nobby.

Ronnie No! We can sort this. Once it's got new plates no one will know.

Jas We'll get it crushed at Den's.

Ronnie I'm ringing it.

Jas We can't! This is really fucked.

Beat.

Ronnie You fucked it! No one deserves to be killed, Jas.

Jas She was gonna rip off the old man, you know that don't you, Nobby. She was gonna take everything he spent his life working for.

Nobby You said it was an accident.

Jas It was.

Ronnie I'm gettin' out of here.

Jas You'd do it Ronnie, you said you would.

Ronnie There's sayin' and doin'. You did and I'm sayin' I'm gone.

Jas You'd do it, Nobby. Your girl walked all over you, she was fuckin' some other bloke when you were wasting your time crying over her. You said you'd kill her, didn't you?

Nobby I ain't hearing this.

Nobby covers his ears and hums loudly to block out any sound.

Jas She took everything you cared about and threw it back in your face, she shat on you. I bet she's laughing at you right now. They all laugh at us.

Moment.

I probably did the old man a favour.

Beat.

She's a fuckin' slag.

Beat.

I followed her to the park. I saw something and I . . . I pressed the brake, I swear it was the . . .

Nobby What did you see?

47

Jas The car didn't stop, it went faster, I couldn't stop, I tried to swerve but I couldn't. She just hit . . . I swear it was the . . .

Ronnie What did you see?

Jas My Mum.

Beat.

Nobby Shit.

Ronnie You've lost it, Jas.

Jas I could smell her in my car.

Jas holds out the dress. Nobby and Ronnie stay their ground.

You believe me don't you, Nobby?

Ronnie Fuck both of you. Did anyone see you nick the car?

Jas No.

Ronnie Did anyone see you run her over?

Jas I don't think so.

Ronnie I'm taking the car.

Nobby We're in this together, Ronnie.

Ronnie Up yours. I'm a young man. There's no way I'm doing time for murder. I didn't do this.

Nobby You're involved.

Ronnie Don't give me that.

Nobby We're mates.

Moment.

Ronnie Give me the keys, Jas.

Beat.

Give them to me!

Jas hands Ronnie the keys. Ronnie takes them. He exits.

Nobby We'll bury her in the garden.

Jas I saw my Mum.

Nobby We'll dig a deep hole.

Jas I was thinking about killing her and stuff but I never meant to do it.

Nobby touches the body gently.

Nobby It's cold . . .

Ronnie bursts in.

Ronnie The wing's dented!

Beat.

You better fix it.

Beat.

Jas? You heard me Jas.

Nobby We're choppin' it.

Ronnie Shut up, you sap.

Jas covers his face with his hands.

Nobby Listen, Ronnie . . .

Ronnie Don't you ever come up against me.

Nobby I ain't . . .

Ronnie I want this car done, now.

The phone rings.

Nobby We'll get caught.

Ronnie I didn't do anything.

Nobby We're in this together.

Ronnie Jas. Oi, Jas!

Ronnie grabs Jas. Nobby tries to stop him. Ronnie slaps Nobby.

Jas gets frustrated and kicks the body. Ronnie stops.

Jas Get up.

He kicks it harder.

Ronnie Alright, enough! You proved your point. I ain't touchin' him. I just want my . . .

Jas kicks it harder.

Jas Get up.

Nobby She's dead.

Jas Get up you slag!

Jas sits astride the body and shakes her.

Answer the phone!

He slaps her harder. The phone rings.

Slag!

The lights buzz and flicker. Jas slaps her again. The phone stops ringing. Moment. Jas begins to pull the clothes off the body.

Ronnie Jas, please. I'm sorry.

Nobby It has to go!

Ronnie No.

Nobby We have to chop it up.

The body is stripped down to the underwear.

Jas Chop her up.

Silence.

Nobby Throw her in the river.

Beat.

Ronnie Put her back in the park. Let the old Bill sort it out.

Nobby Bury her in the garden.

Jas searches around the garage. He finds the electric saw. He stands over the body with the saw in his hands. He kicks the body.

Don't!

Beat.

Jas Kick her, Nobby.

Nobby No.

Jas She can't feel anything.

Ronnie Fuck the car, Jas. I said fuck the car! I'll help you.

Moment.

Jas It's just a piece of meat.

Nobby You're not thinking straight, Jas. Don't make it worse than it is.

Jas It's a piece of meat just like in a butcher's shop.

Ronnie She's a person.

Jas It's dead meat.

Jas switches on the saw. The lights buzz and flicker. The buzzing sound gradually increases. Jas raises the saw over his head.

Ronnie We'll bury her! Nobby, mix some cement.

Nobby Was it three parts . . .

Ronnie Now!

The buzz is very loud. Jas slowly brings the saw down to the body, he stops as it gets very close. The buzz fades. Moment. He switches the saw off.

Jas Get the car in.

Lights fade.

SCENE TWO

9.45 p.m. Garage. Everything is covered in dust. The Porsche's blood-stained wing is leant up against the wall. Nobby sweeps away the dust and debris into black bin liners. Jas stands over the body, covered in sweat with the electric saw in is hand. Enter Ronnie. He wears his trousers and shirt with the sleeves rolled up. He is covered in dust and grease.

Ronnie Give me a hand with the wing, Jas.

Jas doesn't move. Nobby puts down the broom, he moves to the wing. Both carry it out and load it on to the back of the truck. Moment. They enter.

Five grand down the shit hole.

Nobby Had to be done.

Ronnie Not if he didn't fuck it all up it didn't.

Nobby These things happened, Ronnie.

Ronnie These things don't just happen, 'Nobby'. People don't kill people over nothing, 'Nobby'. How many people do you kill every year, 'Nobby'?

Nobby I was only sayin'.

Ronnie Well don't! I don't wanna hear any more crap.

Nobby Be nice, it's his birthday.

Ronnie You fuckin' trippin' or what?

The lights flicker and buzz.

Jas I think we should cut her up.

Pause.

We can put bits of her everywhere, all in different places, no one will work it out.

Ronnie moves to the door.

Ronnie I'm gone.

Nobby You can't.

Ronnie stops.

Ronnie I'll do anything I bloody well want. This ain't my problem.

Jas You told me to do it.

Ronnie Don't . . . Oi! Don't do this, Jas. I didn't ask you to kill anyone.

Jas Same thing.

Ronnie What?

Nobby He's got a point. If you hadn't asked him to get the car, he'd never have killed her.

Ronnie I don't need this. I've got two kids at home.

Jas You helped chop up the car.

Ronnie I'm not chopping up any dead people.

Pause.

Bury her.

Nobby Where?

Ronnie In the pit.

Jas No.

Ronnie We'll put her in and concrete it over. No one will ever know.

Jas Too obvious, everyone does that.

Ronnie How many people do you know under concrete, then?

All move to the body. Moment. They cautiously touch it in order to pick it up.

Mr Jutla (*offstage*) What the bloody hell are you all playing at!

All panic. They look around for a place to hide the body.

Why didn't you pick up the phone?

Ronnie moves to the pit. The other two pick up the body and throw it in. All cover it with the boards. Jutla enters. He wears his blue suit and carries a bottle of whisky and a mobile phone. He is drunk.

Why didn't you drop the car off at the pub?

Jas I didn't have time . . .

Mr Jutla You had all fuckin' day you idiot!

Moment.

Did she call here?

All Three No . . .

Mr Jutla Bloody women. Never trust them. You're talking to an expert . . . I know them like I know the back of my hand. They're trouble . . . You go out of your way to make things nice for them and they don't even bother to show up. Ungrateful bitch . . .

Mr Jutla stares at Jas.

She's probably pissed off because you didn't drop the car off . . . Idiot . . .

Mr Jutla heads for the telephone. He dials a number. Moment. He notices the dust.

What have you bunch of arseholes been doing here?

Pause. Jutla slams the phone down.

Mr Jutla Ronnie, man of the night! Never brings business here during working hours.

Ronnie It was an emergency, Mr Jutla.

Mr Jutla Fuck all this Mr Jutla crap, call me Sid. We're all men in here, aren't we.

Mr Jutla gives Jas a dirty look.

Well, some of us.

Moment.

Mr Jutla Do you bunch of arseholes know what day it is today? It's my son's birthday! Today marks twenty-three years of this bastard's life. Have you had a good twenty-three years, son? Have you?

Jas They've been alright.

Mr Jutla I've given the last twenty-three years over to you, do you know that? 'twenty-three' shit fucking years, and what do I get?

Mr Jutla points to Jas.

This.

The lights buzz and flicker. Jutla looks up at them.

Think it's her don't you, eh? Don't you, son?

Jutla laughs at Jas. He raises the bottle of scotch into the air.

I want us all to share in a birthday drink!

Nobby My Mum's waiting for me to go home, Mr . . . Sid.

Mr Jutla notices the cake. He scoops up a handful and stuffs it into his mouth. Moment.

Mr Jutla No offence intended, Nobby, but your Mother is probably up against some wall behind the Old Queen's Head with her knickers down to her ankles and getting rogered by some drunk. I don't mean to be offensive, Nobby, but we all know what kind of woman she is. Am I right? You know what I'm talking about don't you, my boy?

All three look to the floor in embarrassment.

Come on now, lads. It's me talking here. Me, Sid! This is men's talk. We shouldn't feel ashamed. There aren't any women hanging around to pick us up on our thoughts. We don't have to feel guilty about the way we are. We're men, and proud of it!

Long pause.

(*to Jas*) Get some glasses!

Jas moves to the cupboard and takes out four dusty tea mugs. He cleans then on his overalls and places them on the workbench. Jutla pours out four large whiskys. Jutla raises his glass.

This is for my son and his twenty-three happy years. Cheers!

All take a glass.

Drink!

All three down the whisky in one go. Jutla laughs.

Thirsty, eh?

He pours out another round. All raise their glasses.

Twenty-three years since my wife was taken away from me.

Silence. The glasses are lowered.

I remember her screaming as she gave birth. She held my hand so tightly that her nails were impaled into my palm. There was nothing I could do. She dug them in so deep, blood just poured from my hand. Then I knew she was dead. The doctors delivered a new life but my Rita was dead.

Jutla looks up at Jas.

I held you. You were so small. All I wanted to do was squeeze you. I wanted to squeeze the life out of you and put it back into her.

Moment. Jutla motions Jas to come over to him. Jas cautiously moves to him.

And, you see, this is what I get for all my hard work. This is what I threw the best years of my life away for.

The lights buzz and flicker. Jutla looks up at them and laughs.

You see her, don't you? You feel her around you, don't you? Tell us, what does she feel like? What does she sound like? Is she here?

Jutla laughs.

Jas I remember her bouncing me on her knee in the front room.

Jutla looks at Ronnie and Nobby. All three burst out laughing.

Mr Jutla He remembers that.

Jas As if it was yesterday.

Mr Jutla Yesterday!

All laugh louder.

Well, that's good, that's bloody good. She bounced him on her knee after she died giving birth to the bastard.

The laughter fades. Moment.

Why are you doing this to me?

Jas I'm sure it was real.

Mr Jutla She was my wife, I lost her not you!

Jas But I was only . . .

Jutla slaps Jas hard across the face.

Mr Jutla Don't!

The lights buzz and flicker louder and more frantically than before.

(*to Ronnie and Nobby*) Get out!

Ronnie Hey, Sid . . .

Mr Jutla Mr Jutla to you, boy.

Nobby But maybe we should talk about this . . .

Mr Jutla Get out now, both of you!

Jutla lunges towards them, they move to the door.
Moment.

I want to talk to my son, alone. Please.

Moment.

Jas nods to Ronnie and Nobby, as if to say he's okay.
The guys leave. Jutla slowly moves to the calendar,
takes it off the wall and stares at it. Long pause.
He moves back to the workbench and pours another
drink.

I had to leave a fifty pound deposit and show them my
driving licence before they'd give me the suit back.

Beat.

Have you got a cigarette?

Jas is taken aback by the request but he gives Mr Jutla
a cigarette followed by a light.

Don't smoke much, just the occasional one with a drink.
There's a lot you don't know about me. A lot.

Jutla stares at the calendar. He smiles.

I brought this for your Mother the day she found out she
was pregnant.

Mr Jutla points to the calendar.

You see this mark? This is the day she thought you
would be born. She looked forward to that day, I
remember the look in her eye when she used to talk
about it. She had beautiful eyes.

Jutla looks at Jas for a moment.

When I slapped you . . .

Jas Didn't hurt . . .

Mr Jutla But . . .

Jas It's alright.

Mr Jutla The evil fire-water you understand.

Jas I know.

Mr Jutla When I met her she was so innocent. She was shy. I would have to switch off the light before she undressed. I've never seen such innocence in a woman before, or since. But that soon changed.

Beat.

Short dresses, women's lib, it didn't suit her. I didn't mind you understand, I bought her that black dress, it was pressure from her friends and people at work. She didn't want that, she wanted a quiet life, but we needed the money.

Beat.

All the men used to look at her when she wore that dress. I felt so proud to be walking next to her, that she was mine. You'd think time would heal but I still wake up thinking she's lying next to me.

Jutla takes a long pull from his cigarette. The lights gently buzz and flicker.

Bloody wiring. I've had it done twice.

Moment. Jas sniffs the air.

Jas That smell . . . Can you smell it?

Jutla pours himself out another drink and downs it.

Mr Jutla This has to stop, Jasbir. Please, it's not healthy.

Jas It smells like her dress.

Mr Jutla Forget this nonsense!

The lights buzz and flicker. Moment. They stop. Long pause. Jas heads for the door.

Sit down, let's talk.

Jas is about to exit.

Keep me company. I need company tonight.

Jas waits by the door.

I waited for Linda at the restaurant. She didn't turn up.

Mr Jutla pours himself another drink.

A man of my age needs company. I loved your Mother, I miss her, but a man has to move on. Your Mother would have wanted that, I know she would.

Jutla drinks. Jas silently exits. Jutla does not notice.

I was going to ask her to marry me. I had the champagne on ice and a ring for her finger.

Moment.

She left me sitting on my own. All I could think about was your Mother. If I could go back I would have never . . . I loved your Mother, you know that don't you? I never talked about her because it hurt, but you knew I loved her, you could tell, couldn't you . . . ?

Jutla turns to see that Jas has gone. He throws his mug at the door.

What the bloody hell d'you know about anything! You haven't lived!

Jutla stares at the calendar. He picks it up, and gently strokes it. He cries. A noise from the pit. Mr Jutla is startled. He looks about but cannot see anything.

Bloody place. I nearly had a heart attack. Bloody cats.

Mr Jutla drinks some whisky. The lights buzz, flicker, then blow out. Only the moonlight illuminates the garage. The Dead Woman crawls out of the pit. Mr Jutla hears the sounds and freezes. The woman stands in the shadows, shivering. Moment. She holds the dress in her hand.

Mr Jutla Amrita? . . . Is that you?

Dead Woman I'm cold.

Jutla freezes. Beat.

Look into my eyes. Look!

Mr Jutla looks into the woman's eyes. Moment.

It's cold.

Mr Jutla Amrita . . . ?

The Dead Woman tries to put on the dress, it hurts her to do it, but she continues. Mr Jutla is mesmerised as he looks on.

Dead Woman It hurts so much, Gurmeet. It smells like death. Help me. Help me with the zip, Gurmeet. Please.

Moment.

I've been by your side every night and every day.

Mr Jutla No.

Dead Woman I know you love me. I know you want to be with me.

Mr Jutla My God. Help me . . .

Dead Woman Come to me, Gurmeet. Come.

Moment. Mr Jutla faces her. Dead Woman turns around. Mr Jutla gently zips her up. She turns to face him. She gently hums a tune. Mr Jutla listens for a moment. He softly joins in. They hum together for a moment.

Mr Jutla I prayed for you . . .

Dead Woman . . . Thank you.

Mr Jutla While you were dying.

The Dead Woman gently strokes Mr Jutla's hair. She continues humming.

You look so beautiful in that dress.

Beat.

Mr Jutla I missed you.

Mr Jutla tries to kiss the woman. She abruptly stops humming and pushes him away. Moment. Mr Jutla pours out a large whisky and a very small one. Jutla offers her the small whisky. Moment. She takes the large whisky. Beat. She downs it in one go, then gives the mug back to him. She then moves to the calendar. She looks at it for a moment, then hangs it on the wall. Jutla dusts down the seat and pours her out another small whisky. She takes it.

Dead Woman I'd forgotten how painful it is to be alive. I'd forgotten what it felt like. For years I've been wandering without a voice or a thought. I've been to the stars and know the secrets of the sun. When I was dead I knew everything there is to know.

Mr Jutla You're back now. With me.

The Dead Woman adjusts Jutla's jacket and shirt.

I thought about you night and day for twenty-three years, and now I see your eyes again. You could have lived if you had got rid of it. The pregnancy made you weak.

She pushes him back.

Dead Woman It made me strong.

Mr Jutla I loved you.

Dead Woman You made me weak.

Mr Jutla I thought of you every day.

Dead Woman When I was dead.

Mr Jutla No, always.

Dead Woman I've been by your side. Watching.

Mr Jutla Then you've seen.

Dead Woman You neglected my son.

Mr Jutla My luck has been bad. The business was about to take off, we didn't need a child then.

Dead Woman I did. You neglected all that was real.

Mr Jutla moves away from the Dead Woman. She downs the whisky in one go. Moment.

Another.

She belches.

Please.

Mr Jutla pours her out another.

Mr Jutla You're not real! This isn't real.

She takes Mr Jutla's hand and puts it on her blood-stained face. He looks at his blood-stained hands.

Dead Woman I'm real.

Beat.

Mr Jutla I worked morning until night to clothe and feed you. I was a good husband. I had to work. You know I cared. But I was tired . . . I didn't mean . . .

Moment. Mr Jutla moves to the Dead Woman. She holds her stomach and doubles over in pain. Mr Jutla stops.

Dead Woman I wanted to be with my son, I just wanted to spend a little time with him.

Mr Jutla It was an accident. You're not Amrita. Amrita was sweet and loyal . . .

Dead Woman I wanted to see him grow.

Beat.

Mr Jutla Go!

Dead Woman You prayed for us to be together again. Your God sent me.

Mr Jutla No.

Dead Woman Come to me. Please.

Long pause. Mr Jutla moves towards the woman. He looks into her eyes.

Mr Jutla A man can see a soul.

Dead Woman Would you look after me if I was to come back?

Mr Jutla Yes.

Dead Woman Tell me how it would be.

Pause.

Mr Jutla I would work because I would know there was someone to come home to. I would build you a big house with a big kitchen and anything else you wanted. I would make sure . . .

Dead Woman And Jasbir?

Mr Jutla He's old enough to be out on his own now.

Dead Woman Oh.

Mr Jutla I would hold you and comfort you. My life would be complete again.

Dead Woman Sounds perfect for you.

Mr Jutla It's all I've dreamed about.

Dead Woman What about my dreams? My son?

Beat.

Mr Jutla You look so beautiful in that dress. Do you remember when I brought it for you?

Dead Woman Yes.

Mr Jutla You only wore it once.

Dead Woman You didn't want me to show my legs.

Mr Jutla But you were so beautiful. I was so proud of you when we walked into that restaurant.

Dead Woman You made me look at the floor throughout the whole meal.

Mr Jutla feels the blood on his head. He looks at it, then at the woman. The Dead Woman downs the whisky in one.

Mr Jutla You've got to take it easy, you know what you get like if you drink too much.

Dead Woman Another.

Mr Jutla I think you've had more than enough . . .

She takes a blanket from the pit and wraps it up. She cradles it like a baby, moves to the drawers, opens one and hides the blanket inside.

It was always your baby, that's all you cared about.

She takes the bottle from his hand.

Dead Woman He's ours.

Mr Jutla How do I know that for sure?

She smashes the bottle across Mr Jutla's head. Blood pours out. Moment. Jutla is in shock.

The Dead Woman rummages around in one of the crates, she finds a make-up bag and, using a mirror, she grotesquely smears lipstick on her blood-stained face. She hums a soft tune. Jutla listens, he joins in. Moment.

Dead Woman I missed having a body. Now I'm not too sure.

She looks up at Jutla.

Do you want me?

Moment.

Mr Jutla Yes.

Dead Woman Do you want to make love to me?

Mr Jutla Yes.

Dead Woman Kiss my feet.

Beat. She smears the eye shadow on.

Kiss them.

Jutla slowly gets on his hands and knees. He lowers his head to kiss her feet.

You're pathetic.

Jutla kisses her foot. She kicks him in the face. Jutla holds his nose with both hands. The Dead Woman smudges eyeliner all over her face.

Got any more whisky?

Jutla shakes his head.

Got a cigarette?

Jutla shakes his head.

I had so many dreams.

Mr Jutla We can start again.

Dead Woman You don't understand.

Mr Jutla It's been so lonely without you.

Dead Woman He's my flesh and blood.

Mr Jutla I want you.

Dead Woman You can't have me, Gurmeet. Can't you see?

Mr Jutla I can see you, that's all I need.

Dead Woman I live through our son, once you see that, I'll be with you again.

Mr Jutla Every night I've dreamt of us together. Every morning I wake up thinking you are by my side, but it's always a dream, and I want to die and be with you.

Dead Woman You can't be with me.

Mr Jutla Then I want to die.

Dead Woman Try to understand.

Mr Jutla I love you.

Dead Woman Then look after him!

Beat.

Mr Jutla If this is real, I swear I'll promise to look after both of you for the rest of my days. Don't leave me again, Rita. The boy's mad. He swears he knows you.

Dead Woman He does.

Moment.

I used to come and play with him while you were busy chasing women around town.

Beat.

Mr Jutla I was lonely.

Dead Woman I was resting. You brought me back.

Mr Jutla I'm glad.

Dead Woman You should never bring the dead back.

Mr Jutla I want you.

The Dead Woman smiles.

Dead Woman You don't know me. You never did. You never will.

She hums a tune. Jutla listens. He moves to her. He kisses her on the cheek. She does not resist. Moment. Mr Jutla begins to kiss and maul at the woman's neck. He kisses her face. She does not respond. He becomes passionate.

Mr Jutla I missed you.

Mr Jutla lies the woman down. She does not respond. He has sex with her. She lies still. Jas enters.

I love you Amrita . . . I love you.

Moment. The woman's body lies still. Mr Jutla pulls his trousers up.

Jasbir . . . She's come back. Your mother has come back to us.

Moment. Mr Jutla turns to the body. It is lifeless.

Amrita . . . ?

Beat.

Long moment. Jas slowly moves to Jutla, he looks down at him. Jutla looks up at Jas.

Jas Mum's dead.

Jas helps Jutla up to his feet. Jutla stares into Jas's eyes. Both carefully pick up the body and place it in the pit. They cover it up.

Mr Jutla I'm sorry, son.

Blackout.

faber and faber

Discover the brightest and best in fresh theatre writing with Faber's new *StageScripts*.

Sweetheart by Nick Grosso
'His ear for the youthful argot is acute, his individual scenes vivid. **Sweetheart** looks good and sounds good.' *Evening Standard*

Mules by Winsome Pinnock
'A fascinating, kaleidoscopic look at black female drug smugglers shuttling between Jamaica and London.' *Observer*

The Wolves by Michael Punter
'Punter not only writes beautifully and intelligently, but he plays on the very idea of language. It is an exceptionally meaty début.' *Guardian*

Gabriel by Moira Buffini
'This is a richly themed, enthralling new play.' *The Times*

Skeleton by Tanika Gupta
'This is a touchingly comic and humane drama.' *Independent*

The Cub by Stephanie McKnight
'Clever and sharply observed new writing.' *The List*

Fair Game by Rebecca Prichard
(a free adaptation of **Games in the Backyard** by Edna Mazya)

An afternoon which begins with children's games on the swings escalates into scenes of emotional and physical violence.

Crazyhorse by Parv Bancil
Jas Jutla's life of petty crime descends into darker territory as events spiral out of control and a vengeful spirit enters the house of Jutla.

All Faber *StageScripts* are priced at £4.50.
If you cannot find them stocked at your local bookshop please contact Faber Sales Department on 0171 465 0045.